FAMILIES AROUND THE WORLD

A family from
GUATEMALA

Julia Waterlow

RSVP

RAINTREE
STECK-VAUGHN
PUBLISHERS
The Steck-Vaughn Company

Austin, Texas

FAMILIES AROUND THE WORLD

A family from **BOSNIA**

A family from **BRAZIL**

A family from **CHINA**

A family from **ETHIOPIA**

A family from **GERMANY**

A family from **GUATEMALA**

A family from **IRAQ**

A family from **JAPAN**

A family from **SOUTH AFRICA**

A family from **VIETNAM**

The family featured in this book is an average Guatemalan family. The Calabays were chosen because they were typical of the majority of Guatemalan families in terms of income, housing, number of children, and lifestyle.

Cover: The Calabays outside their home with all their possessions
Title page: The Calabays stand in front of some of the bright cloth made and sold by the local people.
Contents page: Lucia washing the family's clothes at the side of Lake Atitlan

Picture Acknowledgments: All the photographs in this book were taken by Miguel Luis Fairbanks. The photographs were supplied by Material World/Impact Photos and were first published by Sierra Club Books in 1994 © Copyright Miguel Luis Fairbanks/Material World. The map artwork on page 4 was produced by Peter Bull.

© Copyright 1998, text, Steck-Vaughn Company

Published by Raintree Steck-Vaughn Publishers, an imprint of Steck-Vaughn Company

Library of Congress Cataloging-in-Publication Data
Waterlow, Julia.
A family from Guatemala / Julia Waterlow.
p. cm.—(Families around the world)
Includes bibliographical references and index.
Summary: Text and photographs present the home life and day-to-day activities of the Calabays, who live in the mountains of Guatemala.
ISBN 0-8172-4903-6
1. Guatemala—Social life and customs—Juvenile literature.
2. Family—Guatemala—Juvenile literature.
[1. Family life—Guatemala. 2. Guatemala—Social life and customs.]
I. Title. II. Series: Families around the world.
F1463.5.W38   1998
306.85'097281—dc21   97-9996

Printed in Italy. Bound in the United States.
1 2 3 4 5 6 7 8 9 0 02 01 00 99 98

Contents

Introduction

Guatemala is a country in Central America.

REPUBLIC OF GUATEMALA

Capital city:	Guatemala City
Size:	42,042 sq. mi. (108,890 sq. km.)
Number of people:	10,600,000
Main language:	Spanish. There are also about 20 different Mayan languages.
People:	About half are Maya. Some are white, descendants of Spanish people. Others are a mixture of Maya and Spanish.
Religion:	Mainly Roman Catholic. Some people follow the old Mayan religion.
Currency:	Quetzal

THE CALABAY FAMILY

Size of household:	five
Size of home:	215 sq. ft. (20 sq. m.)
Workweek:	Vicente: 60 hours Lucia: "Constant!"
Most valued possessions:	Lucia: Religious painting Vicente: Cassette player Mario: Football
Family income:	$994 each year

The Calabays are an ordinary Maya family who live in Guatemala. The Calabays have put everything they own outside their home so that this photograph could be taken.

Meet the Family

1 Vicente, father, 29
2 Lucia, mother, 25
3 Mario, son, 8

4 Olivia, daughter, 6
5 Maria, daughter, 4

MAYAS

The Maya have lived in Guatemala for thousands of years. Some Guatemalans are a mixture of Spanish and Maya because the Spanish conquered Guatemala in 1523. Today, many people speak Spanish but the Maya have their own languages as well.

The Calabays live on the side of a hill, high in the mountains of Guatemala. Below their house is their village, San Antonio de Palopó, and a lake, Lake Atitlan. The Calabay family has always lived here, farming small plots of land to grow food.

"It doesn't take us long to walk down to the village, but coming up the hill again is hard work when we're carrying things."—*Vicente*

The Calabay House

On the side of the house is a little shed. Inside is the newest thing the Calabays own—a white toilet.

A Home of Their Own

The Calabays saved to buy their own house. It is made of mud bricks and has a tin roof. They have one room inside that Vicente painted white to make it bright and cheerful. The family also has a small building beside the house, where they cook and store their food. They don't have a faucet, so Lucia collects water in plastic containers. The family usually goes down to the lake to wash.

"We have one room, which we use for weaving, eating, and sleeping." —*Lucia*

The Calabays don't have a lot of things in the house. There are a few pieces of furniture, their clothes, the looms they use for weaving, and tools for farming—all things that they can't do without. They also have a cassette player and a few toys for the children.

The Calabays have a bed, a table, and a mat on the floor. Lucia has decorated the walls with some pictures.

▲ At night, the children curl up together with their toys.

Tucked in Safe at Night

The Calabays sleep together in their one room. The children sleep on a mat on the floor, and Vicente and Lucia have a bed. To be on the safe side, they lock the door at night to keep out thieves. But no one has ever tried to break in.

11

Cooking and Eating

TASTY TORTILLAS

In Guatemala, people eat tortillas rather than bread. Tortillas are made of flour and water mixed together. The mixture is rolled out into thin, round pancakes. They are cooked in a big flat pan over the fire.

This is the cookhouse where Lucia prepares all the family's meals.

Tortillas

Lucia puts a big pan on the fire, adds a little oil and fries the tortillas. The Calabays have tortillas with all their meals.

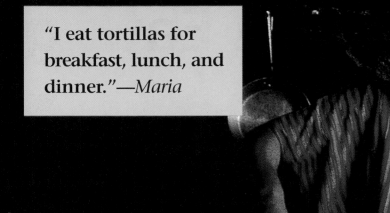

"I eat tortillas for breakfast, lunch, and dinner."—*Maria*

Lucia cooks the family's meals on a fire in the corner of their cookhouse. She has made the fireplace out of stones and puts her cooking pots on top. Lucia hangs her pans and baskets on the walls when she's not using them.

The cookhouse doesn't have a chimney, so the smoke from the fire makes the walls of the cookhouse black.

Maria and Lucia in the cookhouse making lunch

Hot and Spicy

The Calabays grow most of the food they eat. They go to the market in the nearby town of Solola to buy food they can't grow themselves. Lucia uses flour made out of corn to make tortillas and tamales. Often Lucia adds chilies to the food, which makes it spicy.

At breakfast, the family sometimes has scrambled eggs. At midday, they often eat beans and rice. In the evening, one of their favorite meals is beans and tamales. And, of course, with every meal the Calabays have tortillas!

The local market sells all kinds of fruits and vegetables.

Lucia is making tamales, which are like cakes made of flour with a spicy filling. She wraps them in leaves and steams them.

Working Hard

FARMING THE LAND

Most people in Guatemala are farmers. They grow enough food to feed their families and sometimes a little extra to sell at the market. A few Guatemalans work for big landowners, who grow crops such as coffee and bananas.

The Calabays have two looms and a spinning wheel. Vicente uses the largest loom to weave blankets.

Weaving

Vicente weaves blankets for the village shop. The shelves of brightly colored blankets reach to the ceiling. Many tourists visit Lake Atitlan and buy blankets to take home as souvenirs.

"It takes me several days to weave a blanket."—*Vicente*

Vicente hoes the ground, so it is ready for planting more vegetables.

Farming

Vicente is also a farmer. He works with a few simple tools, such as the hoe he uses to clear his fields of weeds. He also has three very sharp machetes for cutting down tough plants. Vicente walks every day to work on fields on the slopes rising from the lake. Mario sometimes goes with his father.

Housework

After each meal, Lucia washes the pots and pans with water she has brought from the lake. If the weather is good, she likes to do this outside.

"Jon Pipin," the family pet turkey, watches Lucia to see if there are any scraps of food.

Lucia keeps busy taking care of the family. Apart from washing the dishes, she chops wood for the fire every day. Lucia also goes down to the lake to collect water or to wash the clothes.

Lucia washes the family's clothes in the lake. It's hard work, but there is a beautiful view of the mountains.

Things to Sell

There is always plenty for Lucia to do. Lucia and her friends sometimes sort the onions they have grown. They tie them into neat bundles, ready for sale at the market in Solola. When Lucia has some spare time, she uses the spinning wheel or the smaller of the two looms. She makes wristbands and bags to sell to tourists.

Lucia wraps onions into bundles to take to market and catches up on the local gossip.

21

School and Play

These are the children's favorite toys.

Most children in Guatemala go to elementary school, but not many go on to secondary school. A lot of families don't have enough money. They need their children to help work on the land when they get older.

Learning to Read

Mario and Olivia go to the local school in San Antonio. They walk together down the hill to school early in the morning. Lucia is glad that her children are learning to read and write. Vicente can read and write, but Lucia never went to school.

Soccer Crazy

If it's wet outside after school, the children play inside the house. They don't have a television set but they find other things, such as drawing, to do. The girls have fun playing with their dolls. Mario is crazy about soccer. He spends nearly all his spare time kicking his ball around.

▼ Mario and his classmates at school

Spare Time

▶ The cassette player is very important to Vicente.

▼ Vicente catches up on the local news.

Time to Relax

Vicente and Lucia don't have much time to sit down and relax. But if Lucia's friends drop in while she's doing something, she always stops to talk to them. Vicente loves listening to the radio when he's not working. Sometimes he sits down and reads the local newspaper.

"I often fall asleep on the bus on the way to market."—*Olivia*

Off to Market

The Calabays travel on a bus to the market.

The Calabays go to the market once a week. They go to Solola, which isn't far away. The road is a bit bumpy, so it can take the bus an hour to get there. Lucia does her weekly food shopping there.

A Religious Family

Lucia is very religious. She often goes to pray at an altar to the village saint, San Antonio del Monte. On the altar there are candles, religious pictures, and flowers. Each year a different family in the village is allowed to have the altar in its house. Lucia believes that the saint looks after their village.

Lucia and other villagers pray at this altar. It is kept at a neighbor's house.

"Our biggest festival is our saint's day in June. Everyone comes out on the streets to watch the colorful parades."
—Lucia

The Future

Vicente and Lucia would like the children to stay at school for many more years. But as soon as Mario, Olivia, and Maria are old enough, they will need to help with all the work. Mario wants to be a farmer and weaver like his father.

The Calabays are happy with their work and way of life. Of course, it would be nice to have more money. Most of all, they would like to have a television set.

Mario likes reading. But he will soon have to leave school to help his father.

"It would be nice to have some new things for the house."—*Lucia*

Pronunciation Guide

Atitlan	Eye-**teet**-lun
Calabay	**Kah**-lah-buy
Guatemala	Gwa-tah-mah-lah
Lucia	Loo-**chee**-uh
Mayan	**My**-un

Quetzal	**Kwet**-zul
Tamale	Tah-**mah**-lee
Tortillas	Tor-**tee**-yah
Vicente	Vih-**chen**-tay

Glossary

Altar A table with religious things on it where people come to pray.

Chili Small vegetable with a very hot taste.

Christian Someone who follows the religious teachings of Jesus Christ.

Corn A cereal crop. Some types of corn can be dried and ground to make flour.

Independent country A country that rules itself and is not controlled by another country.

Looms Wooden frames that are used for weaving.

Machetes Sharp, heavy knives used for cutting down plants.

Spinning wheel A special wheel used to make long threads out of wool.

Volcanoes Cone-shaped hills or mountains where hot rocks from deep under the earth have pushed up violently to the surface.

Weaving Making cloth by threading strands of cotton in and out of each other.

Books to Read

Cummins, Ronnie. *Guatemala*. Milwaukee, WI: Gareth Stevens, 1990.

Lerner Publications Department of Geography Staff. *Guatemala in Pictures*. Minneapolis, MN: Lerner Publications, 1987.

Malone, Michael. *Guatemalan Experience*. Minneapolis, MN: Lerner Publications, 1996.

Index